Thank Heavens for Cats

To....

May God bless you with a loving cat to enrich
your life, to share your home and to warm your heart.

From...

Romans 11:36
For all things were created by him,
and all things exist through him and for him.
To God be the glory for ever!
Amen.

(Good News Translation)

God gave us cats to enrich our lives

In the beginning, God created man,
but seeing him so feeble, He gave him the cat.

Warren Eckstein
American animal trainer, 1949–present day

What greater gift than the love of a cat?

Charles Dickens
English writer, 1812–1870

Time spent with cats is never wasted.

Sigmund Freud
Austrian psychologist, 1856–1939

Psalm 103:5
He fills my life with
good things...
(Good News Translation)

2

Time spent with a purring cat is an investment in happiness, comfort and companionship.

God gave us cats to be our companions

Our perfect companions never have
fewer than four feet.

Colette
French novelist, 1873–1954

When I play with my cat,
how do I know that she is not passing
time with me rather than I with her?

Michel de Montaigne
French philosopher, 1533–1592

Psalm 107:1
Give thanks to the LORD,
for he is good...
(New International Version)

God gave us cats to make us smile

Cats are a tonic, they are a laugh,
they are a cuddle, they are at least
pretty just about all of the time,
and beautiful some of the time.

Roger Caras
American author of A Cat is Watching, *1928–2001*

I have noticed that what cats most
appreciate in a human being is not
the ability to produce food
which they take for granted,
but his or her entertainment value.

Geoffrey Household
English author of Rogue Male, *1900–1988*

No one can stay
serious for long when
faced with a group
of slipping, sliding,
clambering, climbing
kittens.

Look at this, I have perfected the art of cute!

God gave us cats to improve our health

Owning a cat is good for your heart. Studies have discovered that stroking a cat has a positive calming effect which can lower your stress level and reduce high blood pressure.

•

A meow massages the heart.

Stuart McMillan
Scottish politician, 1972–present day

If purring could be encapsulated, it would be the most powerful anti-depressant on the market.

Claire Grant: Merlin

Cats are great therapists

A cat purring on your lap is more
healing than any drug in the world,
as the vibrations you are receiving
are of pure love and contentment.

Saint Francis of Assisi
Italian Roman Catholic friar and preacher, 1181–1226

Some of the best therapists have
fur, four legs, a silky tail and a
heart-warming purr.

Anon

There are two means of refuge from
the miseries of life: music and cats.

Albert Schweitzer
French-German theologian and philosopher, 1875–1965

Cats help you de-stress ...

There's nothing like a sleeping cat to fill a home with a sense of calm and tranquillity.

●

You can't look at a sleeping cat and feel tense.

Jane Pauley
American journalist, 1950–present day

The ideal of calm exists in a sitting cat.

Jules Renard
French dramatist, 1864–1910

A cat is a dreamer whose philosophy is to sleep and let sleep.

Hector Hugh Munro
British novelist, 1870–1916

Kittens are born with their eyes shut. They open them in about six days, take a look around, then close them again for the better part of their lives.

Stephen Baker
American writer and author of How to Live with a Neurotic Cat

I'm not asleep, I'm in energy-saving mode.

Cats accept us just the way we are...

A cat doesn't care if you're young or old,
A cat doesn't care if your house needs dusting.
A cat doesn't care if you stay in your pyjamas all day,
A cat doesn't care about designer labels.
A cat doesn't care if you're having a bad hair day,
A cat doesn't care if you spend hours watching daytime TV
A cat just wants to share a little quality time with you.

●

You can tell your cat anything and he'll still love you.
If you lose your job or your best friend, your cat
will think no less of you.

Helen Powers
American writer, 1925–present day

Happiness is a comfy chair,
a good book and a warm cat.

Cats are awesome

Even the smallest kitten is a wonderful
masterpiece of God's creation.

•

In the animal world, cats are the
awesome aristocracy.

Anon

Among animals, cats are the top-hatted,
frock-coated statesmen going about their
affairs at their own pace.

Robert Stearns
American pastor and founder of Eagles' Wings

Genesis 1:24–25

Then God commanded, "Let the earth produce
all kinds of animal life: domestic and wild, large
and small" – and it was done. So God made
them all, and he was pleased with what he saw.

(Good News Translation)

Cats are amazing

There is no such thing as 'just a cat'.

Robert A. Heinlein
American writer, 1907–1988

God made the cat in order to give man
the pleasure of caressing the tiger.

Fernand Méry
French author of Just Cats, 1897–1984

A thing of beauty, strength and grace lies
behind that whiskered face.

Jo Kittinger
from The Joy of Cats

I am quite simply
the cat's whiskers!

Cats rule, 'cos cats are cool!

Cats are cool

Cats speak the language of comfort
and coolness and therefore we feel
comfortable and cool whenever
we see a cat!

Mehmet Murat Idan
Turkish playwright, 1965–present day

My husband said it was him or
the cat...I miss him sometimes.

Anon

Women and cats will do as they
please, and men and dogs should
relax and get used to the idea.

Robert A. Heinlein
American writer, 1907–1988

Look at me,
I'm learning to tell the time.

Cats are ins-purr-ational

Cats teach us that life is enthralling,
enchanting, entertaining, exciting,
exhilarating and quite simply...
just plain fun.

•

When bored, find a little cat and
watch it; when very bored, find two
little cats and watch them!

Mehmet Murat Idan
Turkish playwright, 1965–present day

Cats are understanding

Cats know when you are sad
or upset. They sit beside you in quiet,
sympathetic silence, ready to offer
comfort in the shape of a
hug or a listening ear.

Books are great, but I prefer a good cat-alogue!

Cats are wise

I have studied many philosophers and many cats. The wisdom of cats is infinitely superior.

Hippolyte Taine
French critic and historian, 1828–1893

There are many intelligent species in the universe. They are all owned by cats.

Anon

Cats are a mysterious kind of folk – there is more passing in their minds than we are aware of.

Sir Walter Scott
Scottish novelist and poet, 1771–1832

Kind old ladies assure us that cats are often the best judges of character. A cat will always go to a good man, they say...

Virginia Woolf
English author of Jacob's Room, 1882–1941

Cats are smart

Cats can work out mathematically the exact place
to sit that will cause most inconvenience.

Pam Brown
Australian poet and author of Love Cats, 1948–present day

A cat is more intelligent than people believe,
and can be taught any crime.

Mark Twain
American writer, 1835–1910

When my cats aren't happy,
I'm not happy. Not because I care about
their mood but because I know they're just
sitting there thinking up ways to get even.

Percy Bysshe Shelley
English poet, 1792–1822

Cats are smarter than dogs. You can't get
eight cats to pull a sled through snow.

Jeff Valdez
American producer and writer, 1956–present day

You can keep a dog; but it is the cat who
keeps people, because cats find humans
useful domestic animals.

George Mikes
*Hungarian-born British author of How to be an Alien,
1912–1987*

Cats are superior beings

Cats as a class, have never completely got over the snootiness caused by the fact that in Ancient Egypt they were worshipped as gods.

P G Wodehouse
English author of My Man Jeeves, *1881–1975*

The cat could very well be man's best friend, but would never stoop to admitting it.

Doug Larson
American journalist, 1926–present day

For a man to truly understand rejection, he must first be ignored by a cat.

Anon

Dogs have owners, cats have staff.

Anon

Dogs come when they're called; cats take
a message and get back to you later.

Mary Bly
American professor of English Literature, 1962–present day

Cats will amusingly tolerate humans
only until someone comes up with a tin opener
that can be operated with a paw.

Terry Pratchett
English author of Men at Arms, *1948–2015*

Imogen Tate: Fudge

The Cat's 10 Commandments
for human servants

I am your cat and you must wait on me 24/7.

Thou shalt love no other pet more than me.

Thou shalt not shout at me, or be cross with me.

Thou shalt not steal or hide my favourite toys.

Remember my food bowl and keep it
filled with choice treats.

Honor my every whim and always keep your lap ready for me.

Thou shalt not turn away my gifts of dead mice and birds.

Instead, thou shalt praise me for
everything I bring into the house.

Thou shalt not make a fuss of the neighbour's cat,
nor the neighbour's dog, nor any other pet
belonging to the neighbour.

Always remember that I am Top Cat,
the most important animal in your household.

Cats make a house a home

It is a truth universally acknowledged that a man in possession of a warm house and a well-stocked fridge must be in want of a cat.

Heather Hacking
English artist and author of How Cats Conquered the World

I love cats because I enjoy my home;
and little by little, they become its visible soul.

Jean Cocteau
French writer, 1889–1963

A home without a cat, and a well-fed, well-petted and properly revered cat, may be a perfect home, perhaps; but how can it prove its title?

Mark Twain
American writer, 1835–1910

It's really my house, the humans just pay the mortgage.

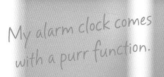

My alarm clock comes
with a purr function.

Cats help us get up on time!

My cat has an internal clock.
Every morning, she wakes me up
before my alarm goes off.
I just wish she understood the
purpose of weekends!

•

There is no snooze button on a cat
who wants breakfast.
Anon

Cats make life better

Every life should have nine cats.

Anon

Cats have a special way of filling
a hole in our lives that we didn't
even know we had!

•

Cats are people, and the
sooner the world accepts that fact,
the better off the world will be.

Harry Allen Smith
American author of Rhubarb, *1907–1976*

Cats are an example to us all

With their qualities of cleanliness, discretion, affection, patience, dignity, and courage, how many of us, I ask you, would be capable of becoming cats?

Fernand Méry
French author of Just Cats, 1897–1984

Cats are intended to teach us that not everything in nature has a purpose.

Garrison Keillor
American radio personality, 1942–present day

You now have learned enough to see that cats are much like you and me...

T.S. Eliot
British author of The Addressing of Cats, 1888–1965

40

I charge extra for purring.

Cats are practically purr-fect in every way

Cats make one of the most satisfying sounds in the world: they purr... a purring cat is a form of high praise, like a gold star on a test paper. It is reinforcement for something we would all like to believe about ourselves – that we are nice.

Roger Caras
American author of A Cat is Watching, *1928–2001*

Purring is an automatic safety valve device for dealing with happiness overflow.

Anon

To err is human, to purr is feline.

Robert Byrne
American author, 1930–2016

The smallest feline is a masterpiece.

Leonardo da Vinci
Italian mathematician, artist and scientist, 1452–1519

Revelation 4:11
You are worthy, our Lord and God,
to receive glory and honour and
power, for you created all things,
and by your will they were created
and have their being.
(New International Version)